THE
Archive Photographs
SERIES

KING EDWARD'S SCHOOL
BIRMINGHAM

SH

'Our pious founder and benefactor', King Edward VI. This portrait was purchased by the Governors in the eighteenth century for £2.

THE
Archive Photographs
SERIES

KING EDWARD'S SCHOOL

BIRMINGHAM

Compiled by
Tony Trott

TEMPUS

First published 2001
Copyright © Tony Trott, 2001

Tempus Publishing Limited
The Mill, Brimscombe Port,
Stroud, Gloucestershire, GL5 2QG

ISBN 0 7524 2448 3

Typesetting and origination by
Tempus Publishing Limited
Printed in Great Britain by
Midway Colour Print, Wiltshire

Birmingham in 1640, eighty-eight years after the foundation of King Edward's School.

Contents

Acknowledgements

I am indebted to the National Portrait Gallery for permission to reproduce photographs of the portraits of Sir John Banks and John Hough on p. 10 and of John Somers on p. 11; to the Birmingham Museum and Art Gallery for permission to print a photograph of the bust of David Cox on p. 16; and to Christopher Tolkien for permission to print the photographs of his father, Professor J.R.R. Tolkien, on pp. 38 and 39.

I have been helped by many people in compiling this collection of pictures and I would like to thank them all: Mrs Lesley Horton; Mr Fred Rogers; many former colleagues who have been able to provide identification of boys unknown to me; and Old Edwardians who have sent me photographs: Robert Anchor, John Corbett, David Crigman, Robert Darlaston, Tom Freeman, Frank Hearne, Hugh Houghton, A.V. Oliver, John Roberts.

I have been unable to locate the holders of the estate of the late Mrs Kathleen Tynan to request permission to print the photograph of Ken Tynan on p. 126. It is, however, such an expressive photograph and he was such a remarkable and distinguished Old Edwardian, that I could not bring myself to leave it out. I hope that no-one will be offended.

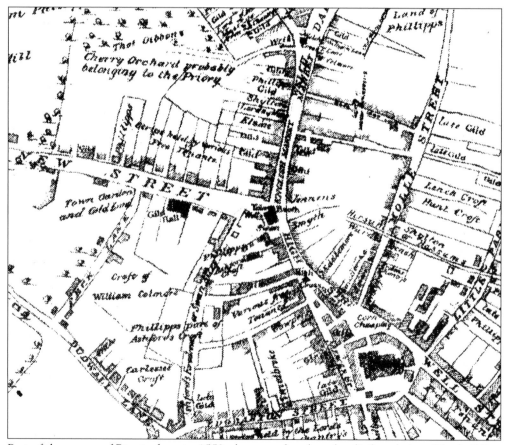

Part of the manor of Birmingham in 1553, the year after the school's foundation. The building marked *Guild Hall* in New Street was the site of the school until 1935.

Introduction
A Brief History of King Edward's School

In 1547 religious guilds were suppressed throughout the country by an Act of Parliament and their assets 'given to the King's majesty'. Among them was the Guild of the Holy Cross in Birmingham. But the Act of Suppression allowed guilds which supported a school to retain lands with an annual value of £20 to continue to support their school. The Guild of the Holy Cross supported no school, yet its leading members petitioned the government to be allowed to reclaim land valued at the statutory £20 in order to *found* one. Surprisingly, this petition was successful, so how did it come about? It came about because the guild had the ear of the lord of the manor of Birmingham who happened to be the Earl (later Duke) of Northumberland, at that time the most powerful man in the country. Birmingham got its school, not from the charity of a pious benefactor, nor from the generosity of a local-lad-made-good but from the enterprise and opportunism of the town's leading citizens who were quick and bold enough to push their luck with the powers that be. Probably alone among all the other schools whose foundation is associated with Edward VI, King Edward's School, Birmingham, was a genuinely *new* foundation and not, as the others were, a *re*-foundation.

The charter of the 'free Grammer Schole' of King Edward VI was issued on 2 January 1552 and the school began its life in what had been the former guild building at the lower end of New Street. In 1596 the governors issued rigorous 'Statutes and Ordinances' but these were not confirmed by the bishop. Throughout the first century of the school's existence the governors were involved in a succession of law suits. The first, in 1604, derived from faction fighting among themselves, between the powerful Colmore and Smalbroke clans. The next two, in 1633 and 1638 respectively, were brought about by complaints concerning their administration of the foundation. Nor did the school escape involvement in the political tension of the mid-seventeenth century. The governors were associated with the town and the town was strongly Parliamentarian, whereas the local gentry – the Holte family of Aston Hall – were, not surprisingly, Royalist. This tension continued until the end of the century, the second half of which saw the emergence of the school's first really commanding and creative headmaster, Brokesby. He led the school with energy and imagination for thirty-six years (1649-1685). We learn that by the 1680s there were 'neer' 200 boys in the school and that a Petty School, a sort of feeder school for the grammar school, had been established.

The affairs of the school in the first two decades of the eighteenth century were dominated by a long-running quarrel between two larger-than-life characters: a powerful, domineering governor called Eden and an irascible and violently Whiggish headmaster called Parkinson. The result of this turbulence was a Royal Commission which reported very unfavourably on the school in 1723. Yet between 1731 and 1734 an elegant new building was erected on the same site in New Street, largely in the absence of the headmaster, Mainwaring, who had an ecclesiastical living elsewhere and allowed the school to be run (perfectly competently) by the usher (second master) and his assistant.

From quite early in the school's history some Birmingham citizens had desired a more practical education for their sons than a grammar school offered so in the second half of the eighteenth century the governors created four elementary schools in various parts of the town to cater for this need. In 1794 they added a fifth for girls.

In the first three decades of the nineteenth century the school continued in what was still an eighteenth-century mould under 'Butcher' Cooke. But in 1834 the appointment of a young headmaster and the decision to erect a new school building, still on the same site, brought about great changes. The new building, in the Gothic style, designed by Barry (subsequently the architect of the House of Commons) was to be a landmark in Birmingham for the next hundred years. The new headmaster, Francis Jeune, was a tough disciplinarian but his most important achievements were in the radical plans he drew up for the reorganization of the school, expanding the curriculum, increasing staff numbers and creating a pension scheme. His tenure was short (1834-1838) but his influence far-reaching.

The Victorian era saw a succession of four very impressive headmasters: Prince Lee (1838-1848); Gifford (1848-1862); Evans (1862-1872); and Vardy (1872-1900). The first of these numbered a future archbishop, two bishops, a future president of a Cambridge college and a future headmaster of the school among his pupils. He also set a new style of headmastering, 'headmaster as guru', that was to predominate in the school for ninety-odd years. It was during this period that the school acquired a national reputation because a considerable number of its old boys became men of importance and influence in academic and public life.

Within the school itself three major developments took place during this period: games became an important feature of school life; mathematics and science achieved equal importance to classics; and the Foundation was radically extended, a development which culminated in 1883. Fee-paying was introduced and a High School for Girls and five other grammar schools created and, most important of all, it was decided after much negotiation that the governing body should include eight members of the Town Council.

In 1900 Vardy was succeeded by Cary Gilson (1900-1929), who was to become one of the school's most impressive and well-loved headmasters. He gathered a strong common room around him and during his time the school became a symbol of success and stability. The financial responsibility for seven schools, however, was proving too much for the Foundation's resources and help had to be sought from the City Council, a development which reduced the governors' freedom of decision. During the headship of Cary Gilson's successor, E.T. England (1929-1941), difficulties multiplied – the necessary move from New Street to a new building on the present site on the Bristol Road, the fire which destroyed the temporary buildings on that site and then the war and evacuation to Repton.

In the years following the war a new headmaster, C.R. Morris (1941-1948) succeeded in finding a much more satisfactory solution to the Foundation's continuing financial problems by negotiating the school's acceptance as a direct grant school. Both he and his successor, T.E.B. Howarth (1948-1952) were academically brilliant and stimulating and saw their major challenge as restoring the intellectual eminence and success that the school had enjoyed before the war.

The years between the departure of Howarth and the present day have seen a succession of important developments, initiated and seen through by a series of energetic headmasters (who by the mid-1950s were called Chief Masters): Canon R.G. Lunt (1952-1974); F.G.R. Fisher (1974-1982); M.J.W. Rogers (1982-1991); H.R. Wright (1991-1998) and R.M. Dancey (1998-). In 1976 the government phased out the direct grant and the school reverted to fee-paying independence, but with the addition of the Assisted Places Scheme which, as it happens, Fisher had a hand in helping to devise. Throughout this period the school had consistently been one of the top academic schools in the country, on occasion *the* top academic school. There have been new buildings – new science laboratories (1959), a music school (1965), and a language laboratory (1965), a new pavilion at Eastern Road (1963), a sports hall and squash courts (1971), a drama studio (1985), the Art and Design Centre (1990) and computer and IT rooms. Curriculum extensions have embraced economics, information technology, drama and design technology. The number of boys in the school has been considerably increased and numbers in the common room increased also. The common room has welcomed women teachers into its ranks, and they now constitute a healthy proportion of its total membership. The range of games, sports and out of school activities has been enormously extended and the scale, ambition and success of the music and drama departments know no bounds. As the school celebrates its 450th anniversary in 2002, it is buoyant and strong in all departments.

Tony Trott, September 2001

One

The Guild Building and the Georgian School 1552-1838

At its foundation in 1552 the school occupied the building which had been the headquarters of the Guild of the Holy Cross (see the map, p. 6). Unfortunately no representation of this mediaeval building remains, but it has been suggested that the Guild Hall still standing at nearby Henley-in-Arden gives a good idea of what it may have looked like – a simple timber-framed, wattle and daub structure. In 1731 this building was demolished and a new school was built. Surviving drawings of the Georgian school (see p. 12) show an elegant and attractive building that, apart from its comic little clock-tower, was free of pomposity and could well have been a gentleman's house. It was built on the familiar post-Renaissance plan where two wings, projecting from a central block, enclose a courtyard open on the fourth side, in this case fronting New Street.

The seal of the Guild of the Holy Cross (left), from which the school originated, and the seal of the new governors under the new charter of 1685 (right). The old governors were re-instated seven years later.

Sir John Banks. As Attorney General for Charles I he presented the Bill of Information brought against the governors of the school in 1638. (Courtesy of the National Portrait Gallery)

John Hough OE (1651-1743), President of Magdalen College, Oxford, Bishop of Lichfield and later Bishop of Worcester. He successfully resisted James II's attempt to turn him out of the presidency of Magdalen College. (Courtesy of the National Portrait Gallery)

William Wollaston, a prominent member
of the group of theologians who preached
'natural theology'. He taught at King
Edward's School and is the earliest master
whose picture survives.

John Somers, a leading Whig
lawyer, made Lord Chancellor by
William III. He was employed by
the 'old' governors in the fight to
overthrow the 'new' governors at
the end of the seventeenth
century. (Courtesy of the National
Portrait Gallery)

The Georgian building of what was then called the 'Free School', erected in the 1730s. It was used for 100 years before being pulled down in 1833 to make way for Barry's building.

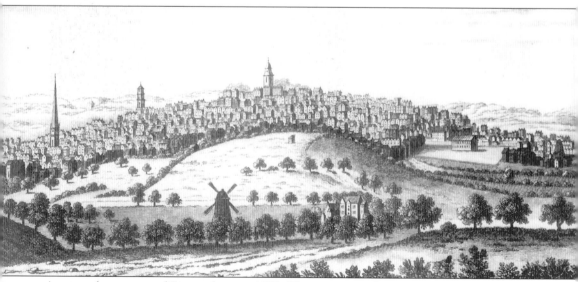

An easterly prospect of Birmingham in 1779. There are now three towers visible (*cf.* p. 4) of which the middle one is that of King Edward's School.

'Great School' in Georgian times, from a watercolour by Samuel Lines.

John Brailsford was headmaster from 1766 to 1773. His main claim to fame is that he is the first headmaster of the school whose likeness we have.

Rann Kennedy taught at KES from 1799 to 1836, the last twenty-eight years as Usher (Second Master). He is shown above as a young man as curate of St Paul's, Handsworth, and, below, after thirty or more years of teaching.

The Georgian school (on the right) in its context, next to the Hen and Chickens Hotel.

John ('Butcher') Cooke, headmaster (1797-1834). It is not certain why he acquired the nickname 'Butcher'.

H.F. Cary, OE, (1772-1834) was the first English translator of Dante. His translation of the *Divine Comedy* became for many years a standard classic.

A portrait bust of David Cox, OE (1783-1859), a leading Birmingham artist of the first part of the nineteenth century. (Courtesy of the Birmingham Museum and Art Gallery)

Two

Barry's Building
1838-1936

A good deal of Francis Jeune's brief but dynamic headmastership (1834-1838) was spent in temporary accommodation because a new school building was being built to take the place of the Georgian school. It was designed by Charles Barry, later to win renown as the architect of the House of Commons, and it was for nearly a hundred years one of Birmingham's greatest buildings. In style it was thorough-going Gothic and as such it was, in the 1830s, in the vanguard of architectural fashion. It was in this building that a succession of powerful headmasters disseminated 'godliness and good learning' and from this building that a succession of Edwardians, who were to achieve a national reputation, embarked on their careers. Its demolition in 1935, though compelled by reason, was a matter of regret and sadness to many OEs of the time and as a result the city lost one of its great landmarks. But the head had ruled the heart and the school left the site that it had occupied for 384 years and moved, lock stock and barrel, to Edgbaston.

The High Street market just by St Martin's in the first half of the nineteenth century. The site of the school in New Street would be just out of the picture to the right.

Francis Jeune, headmaster from 1834 to 1838, from a painting in Pembroke College, Oxford. Jeune's reorganization of the school had a deep and lasting effect.

The legendary James Prince Lee, headmaster from 1838 to 1848. He was a great and inspirational teacher, much revered by a succession of brilliant pupils. He left to become Bishop of Manchester.

Big School in the new building designed by Charles Barry and opened in 1838.

Sapientia, the imposing teaching
desk from which the headmaster
taught the First Class. This was
its original position.

The main entrance to the school
which opened directly on to
New Street and the busy life of
the town.

The Lower Corridor: above, the inside of the main entrance; below, the corridor seen from the entrance door with the staircase to the Masters' Common Room in the right foreground.

The cloisters in the central courtyard, seen from without (above) and within (below).

Edmund Hamilton Gifford, headmaster (1848-62). He came to KES from Shrewsbury School where he had been taught by the famous Benjamin Kennedy, the son of Rann Kennedy (see p. 14).

John Connolly, OE (left 1847), later lieutenant-colonel, was a boarder in Prince Lee's house. He won the Victoria Cross in the Crimean War, after the Battle of the Alma.

Sketches from several sheets
containing twenty-eight
likenesses of masters at the
school in the mid-nineteenth
century.

The artist is not known for certain but it could have been Thomas Clark, appointed 1846. During his time at the school Burne-Jones was a pupil.

(Above) Sidney Gedge, Second Master from 1835 to 1854, successor to Rann Kennedy. The caption to the sketch reads: 'yours till the holidays, S. Gedge'.

Sir Edward Burne-Jones. The famous artist was a pupil at KES during the headmasterships of Prince Lee and Gifford.

Sir Francis Galton, OE (left 1840), was an anthropologist and meteorologist and an explorer in the Sudan and south-west Africa. He also laid the foundations for the science of eugenics.

Charles Evans, OE, headmaster from 1862 to 1872, was one of Prince Lee's most brilliant pupils. He was 'always in a hurry'.

Albert Vardy, headmaster from 1872 to 1900. By patience and determination he brought about the remodelling of the Foundation in the 1880s. His great dictum was that 'schools exist mainly for the average boy'.

The Board Room in Barry's building where governors' meetings were held.

The Art Room in Barry's building.

Joseph Barber Lightfoot, OE (left 1847). He was the most intellectually distinguished of Prince Lee's pupils. He was consecrated Bishop of Durham in 1879.

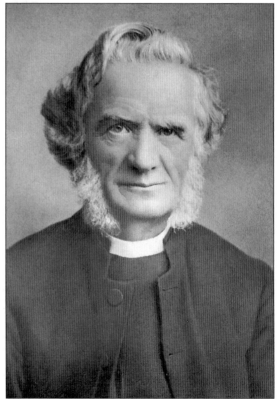

Bruce Foss Wescott, OE (left 1844). He was consecrated Bishop of Durham in 1890. At school he was nicknamed 'Miss Waistcoat'.

Edward White Benson, OE, another of Prince Lee's star pupils. He became Bishop of Truro and later Archbishop of Canterbury.

The head boy of KES and the head girl of King Edward's High School present an address and flowers to Queen Victoria when she visited Birmingham as part of her Golden Jubilee celebrations in 1887.

The KES first XVs of 1892 (above) and of 1894 (below). The master with the 1894 XV is Mr Reynolds.

The school in the latter part of Vardy's headmastership, in the 1890s. The Birmingham of the time is strongly evoked in the picture.

The KES first XI, 1900. White socks were not then essential, and the more dashing cricketers kept their trousers up with a tie.

Rawden Levett (1869-1902) was a great mathematics teacher and, from 1890 onwards, second master. He was described by Cary Gilson as 'probably the best schoolmaster I have ever known'.

Revd John Hunter Smith taught classics between 1861 and 1901. His starting salary was £180 per annum.

Hunter Smith's classroom, June 1895. Smith was a witty, explosive and inspirational teacher, detested by philistines whose prejudices he delighted in demolishing.

A cold day at Eastern Road on Sports Day in 1894.

Robert Cary Gilson, headmaster from 1900 to 1929, was a man of many parts and by all accounts well loved and venerated.

C.H. Heath taught classics from 1900 to 1931 and was one of the original housemasters when houses were first created.

The Common Room in 1906. Notable figures are, on the front row: C. Davidson (second from the left); Cary Gilson (centre); T.J. Baker (extreme right). Middle row: M.J. Acatos (second from the left); C.H. Heath (second from right); A.E. Measures (extreme right). Back row: J. Manton (centre).

The KES first XV of an unknown year in the first decade of the twentieth century. M.C. Harrison (third from right, back row) played for England in 1909 and in 1914. Also in the picture is E.W. Assinder who played for England in 1909.

J.R.R. Tolkien, OE, aged thirteen (left) and his younger brother in 1905.

The KES first XV for the 1910/11 season. J.R.R. Tolkien is on the extreme right of the centre row.

J.R.R. Tolkien, date of photograph unknown. He looks to be either an upper sixth former or an undergraduate.

C. Davidson succeeded to Levett's mathematical empire with his two pupils, Daniels (right) and Ibbotsen (left), each of whom became a Senior Wrangler at Cambridge.

The cast of a production (*c.* 1910) of an unidentified Greek play. The master on the right is A.E. Measures, known later in life as 'The Bulge'.

The combined forces of MI and MIIA, July 1914. The masters are (from left to right) Messrs Whitemore, Langley, Baker and Hodgson.

A group of OE officers during the First World War.

The shooting VIII at Bisley, July 1919. From left to right, back row: Tevens, Turner, Selven, Hale. Front row: Ridley, Capt. Stanton, Incleden, Walker, Murray.

On the march at a cadet camp at Tidbury, 1922. Identifiable are Humphrey, Hirst, Sparsholt, Prow, Mountford, Anderson, Oliver and Capt. Astbury.

The KES cadet corps waiting to board their train for camp at Snow Hill station, *c.* 1925.

Cadet Corps inspection at Eastern Road some time between 1936 and 1939. The inspecting officer is Col. E.G. Gidley-Kitchin and the headmaster in pursuit is E.T. England.

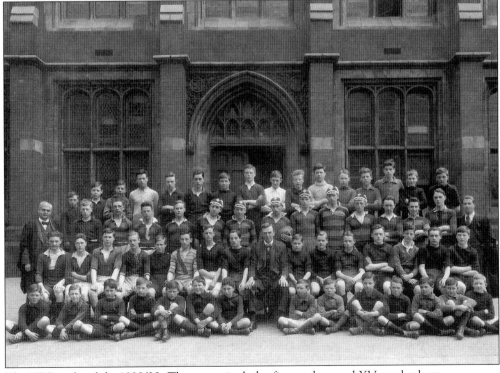

The KES rugby club, 1922/23. The group includes first and second XVs and others.

Edwin England, headmaster from 1929 to 1941. He pressed for the move from New Street to Edgbaston and had to cope with years in the temporary buildings followed by the wartime evacuation.

England and his prefects some time in the 1930s.

Three
The School in Edgbaston 1936 onwards

In January 1936 the school moved into temporary buildings on a new site a few miles from the city centre along the Bristol Road. A main reason for the move had been fire risks in Barry's building so it was a major irony that in May 1936 the temporary buildings were destroyed by fire. New ones had to be built and it was in these that the school functioned while the new school was built. The architect was an Old Edwardian, H.W. Hobbiss, and on an awkward, sloping site he created an attractive complex that embraced buildings for two schools, KES and KEHS. Teaching began in the new school in September 1940, before building work was fully finished. In the sixty years following the opening of the new building much has been added to meet the increase in school numbers and to meet the demands entailed by an ever-expanding curriculum. The situation of the new school, with playing fields, the Winterbourne Gardens and Edgbaston Golf Course all adjacent and the noise and bustle of New Street at a few miles' distance, is open and green and leafy. This makes it a pleasure to learn and teach there.

The temporary buildings along the Bristol Road into which the school moved from New Street in 1936.

Firemen at the scene of the fire that destroyed the temporary buildings in May 1936.

KES boys returning to Birmingham for Christmas 1939 from the 'exile' at Repton where they had been evacuated on the outbreak of war.

A working party engaged in some indefinable activity during the evacuation and supervised by Roger Dunt.

The Cadet Corps band, probably at Repton. The middle figure in the rear rank has been identified as Robert Anchor.

The band back at home in Birmingham, 1940/41.

A rear view of the new buildings at Edgbaston, showing Big School from the back.

The school buildings seen through one of the archways that used to flank the Foundation Office. The archways were removed in the 1980s.

Big School in the process of construction. It was the last part of the building to be completed.

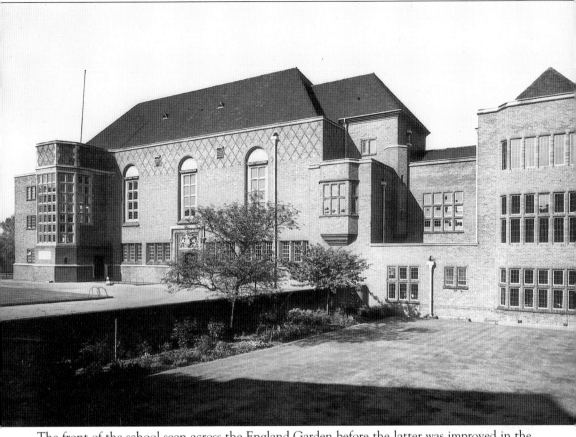

The front of the school seen across the England Garden before the latter was improved in the late 1980s.

KES boys at a farming camp during the Second World War. Exactly what they are doing is not easy to say.

A KES logging camp during the Second World War. The masters in the middle of the centre row are Messrs Sibson (left) and Leeds. To the left of Mr Sibson is Frank Hearne and on the right of Mr Leeds is Ken Dyer. Between them in the back row is Bruce McGowan.

The Prefects in 1940/41, during the acting headmastership (1941-1943) of A.S. Langley, the Second Master.

C.R. Morris, headmaster from 1943 to 1948). The arrival of Morris was delayed for two years until he could be released from his wartime job as Principal Secretary at the Ministry of Supply.

The wartime Common Room, some time between 1943 and 1946. The presence of Morris fixes the first date and the presence of ladies the second.

Sergeant Major William Moore BEM (1918-1953), an unmistakable figure about the school, in charge of PT (as it was then called) and prominent in the Cadet Corps.

Willie Moore supervising a game that looks more like netball than basketball in the immediate post-war years.

William Slim (left 1910), Viscount, KG, GCB, DSO, MC, Field Marshal, Viceroy of Burma, Governor General of Australia, Old Edwardian.

Field Marshal Slim, accompanied by the headmaster, C.R. Morris, and followed by the Second Master, A.S. Langley, arrives down the drive between KES and KEHS.

Tom Howarth, headmaster from 1948 to 1952. He followed his predecessor's example in pepping up the intellectual life of the school after the disruptions of the war.

Tom Burgess (1935-1951), a splendid teacher of classics and English. He moved to become headmaster of King Edward's, Five Ways.

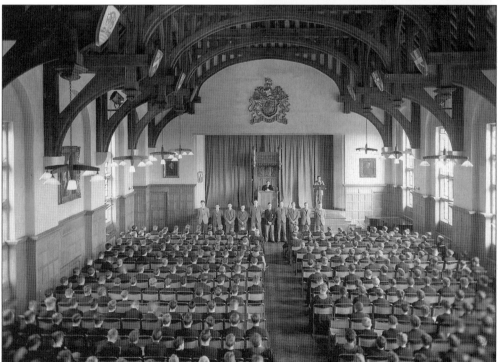

Morning prayers in Big School, 1951. The school captain, on the left of the row of prefects facing the rest of the school, is Paul Gardiner.

The queue for the dining room, probably in 1952/53. Senior boys have not yet been regimented into blazers.

The Common Room in 1951, registering the influx of post-war arrivals.

Boys leaving school down the main drive. Note a rear view of Henry Craddock, second porter, one of the school's most formidable and engaging characters.

Break in the Common Room, some time between 1950 and 1952. From left to right: Dick Osborne, Dyfri Rees, Maurice Porter, Bill Babb, Peter Cadenhead, John Vaughan, Ted Leeds, Robert Cook, John Winnerah.

Activity in the gym, 1940s and 1950s style. The operation is presided over by a fairly youthful John Cotter, a Dunkirk veteran.

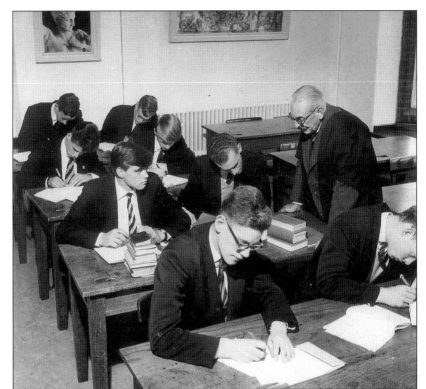

Life in the classroom, 1940s and 1950s style. Above, Roger Dunt teaches the Classical VI or Classical Division and, below, Jack Roberts teaches a Fifth Form maths set.

A school party to France arriving at their destination, possibly Condom, in the early fifties. Masters in charge are Jim Biggs (in the beret) and Ted Leeds.

A school party to Manderscheid, Germany, in the early 1950s, with Bill Barlow, centre, and a large, friendly Dominican on the left.

Ronald Lunt, Chief Master from 1952 to 1974. In his period of office headmasters became known as Chief Masters. Now a legendary figure, he was tireless and dominant.

Canon Lunt and his band of prefects for the year 1955/56. The school captain, Roger Wilson, on the Chief Master's right, captained the victorious KES VII in the Public Schools Seven-a-Side Tournament at Twickenham in 1956.

HM the Queen visited the school in 1955. Here, accompanied by the Chief Master, she looks at a model of the Queen's Beast made by Roger Harper, who just scrapes into the picture.

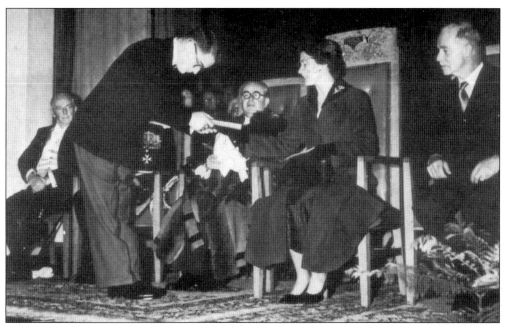

The school captain, Roger Wilson, presents the Queen with a copy of T.W. Hutton's *History of King Edward's School.*

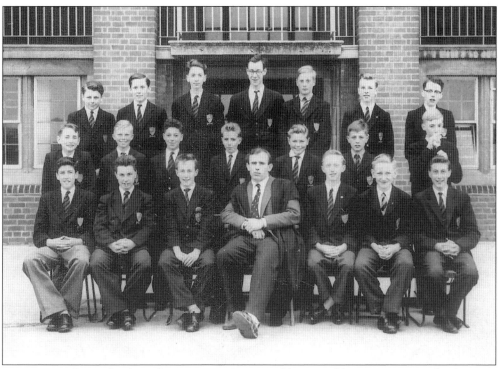

UMD in 1958, with their form master, Peter Robbins. Robbins was an England rugger international, taught French and was given the freedom of the City of Paris. He is slippered because of a foot injury.

Members of the Cartland Club, 1959. The Cartland Club was very much Canon Lunt's creation and comprised prefects, house prefects, members of the first XV and the first XI and a few others. Bill Oddie is behind the Chief Master's right ear.

Cartland Club members of 1954/55 arranged this ironic photograph, centred on the colourful figure of Henry Craddock.

Cartland Club members in the Cartland Room. It is doubtful if sedate chess matches often occupied them in their lair.

Charles Blount, Head of History and school librarian, with his devoted band of helpers, 1958. (Photograph from the collection of R.A. Darlaston, chief library assistant, on the right hand of power in the front row.)

Above, the interior of the school chapel, rebuilt from the Upper Corridor of the New Street building. The painting behind the altar is by Bruce Hurn, head of the art department during the 1950s and 1960s. Below, the exterior.

The old pavilion at Eastern Road. The match in progress is the annual Speech Day fixture between the school first XI and the OE Association XI. The OEs are in the field and the striker looks to be John Barnfield.

Messrs Benson, Everest and Traynor – the nucleus of a good side – at what was probably the annual fixture between the Common Room and the first XI, between 1965 and 1970.

The Chief Master's house, completed in 1958, built to replace the one that stood on the Bristol Road.

The Common Room, 1962.

Graham Underhill (1965-90) and John Hatton (1965-90) along with other Common Room members waiting to be marshalled into position for a school photograph.

Tony Trott rehearses J M Synge's *The Playboy of the Western World*, the end-of-the-year play, in 1978.

The Common Room, 1974.

The Junior Challenge team of 1984: from left to right, Martin Potter, Dougal McCrow, Christopher Nash, Philip Blenkinsop, Matthew Grimley.

The school tuck shop, *c.* 1985. The formidable head porter, Jack Bailey, and his wife, Jean, seek to 'meet customer requirements'.

In 1985 the school was used by the makers of John Cleese's film, *Clockwise*, to shoot a significant part of the film. Here, filming is taking place in Big School.

The Cartland Room was put to better use as the form room of Tom Hosty, Head of English, seen here using an overhead projector to project the text of a poem.

During the 1980s IT became a major factor in the school's curriculum. Stephen Stretton is seen here in action.

By courtesy of KEHS cooking became an option during the 1980s. Above, Ross Yallup enjoys the experience of washing up and, below, Philip Bennett-Britton flips a pancake, observed by Paul Miller.

The portrait of Robson Fisher, Chief Master from 1974 to 1982, was presented by the governors to the school. The painting is flanked on the right by the sitter and on the left by his successor, Martin Rogers, Chief Master from 1982 to 1991.

Hugh Wright, Chief Master from 1991 to 1998.

A group of jolly schoolmasters at Lords on the occasion of the University match in 1997, when Cambridge was captained by Anurag Singh, OE, and Oxford by Mark Wagh, OE. From left to right: Hugh Wright, Simon Tinley, Derek Everest, Tim Jayne, Martin Stead, Lawson Roll, John Hubbard, Keith Phillips, Rick Lye and Matthew Smith.

Roger Dancey, Chief Master since 1998.

The Martin Rogers Design Centre. This impressive new building was opened in 1989/90. Above is an exterior view of the main entrance and below, an interior view.

Work in the Art Room in the new design centre: from left to right Mikaeel Kanani, Mr Bradley Spencer, Andrew Atkinson, George Readings, Sachin Sudera.

Parade ground football has survived periods of official disapproval to continue with unquenchable natural enthusiasm.

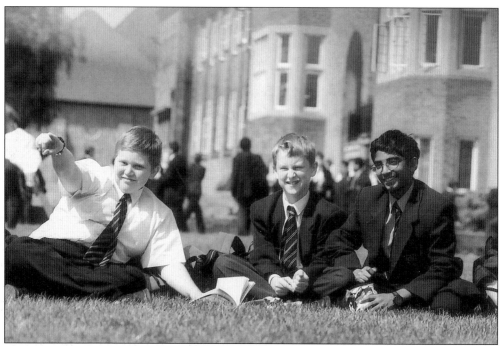

Taking it easy. From left to right, above: Jason Jibrail, Martyn Strong, Arun Anandakumar. Below: Nick Howes, Vikram Gudi, James Cooper.

DRAMA AND MUSIC

John Evans as Sir Epicure Mammon
and James Honeybone as Dol Common
in Tony Trott's production of Ben
Jonson's *The Alchemist* in 1955.

The Second Shepherds' Play, 1958. The
actors are, from left to right, Rodney
Braithwaite, Tony Moreton, Peter
Cairns, Alistair Papps, David Munrow.
Munrow later achieved national fame
as a musician, musicologist and
broadcaster.

Kevin Lee as Desdemona, attended by Michael Gill as Emilia in James Bolton's production of *Othello* in 1966. Lee later became a professional actor and has since become an important dramatist under a slight change of name – Kevin Elyot.

Actors from left to right in this scene from Michael Parslew's 1968 production of John Whiting's *A Penny For A Song* are Michael Cooper, Paul Gompertz and Stuart Atkin.

David Willetts (now an MP) and Robert O'Brien as Antonio and Sebastian respectively are about to murder the sleeping Alonzo when Ariel (Charles Spicer) interposes. This is a rehearsal photograph of Parslew's production of *The Tempest*, 1973.

Chris Evans and George Eletheriou as two very sharp Florentine tradesmen in Kate Barnet's 1985 production of Paul Thompson's *The Lorenzaccio Story*.

A scene from Giles Evans' 1983 production of Sean O'Casey's *Juno and the Paycock*. The actors are, from left to right: Liz Ingham, Paul Davies, Eleanor Crook, Max Carlish, Ken McNab.

A scene from Jenny Herbert's production of *West Side Story*. The actors are, from left to right: Joe Millington, William Grant, Matthew Benjamin, Oliver Scanlan, Richard Benwell, Gareth Price, Simon Plant, Paul Miller.

Hannah Proops and John Carey in Jenny Herbert's 1994 production of *Oklahoma!*

Peter Bridle rehearses the Joint Orchestra in Big School, 1983.

Previous page:
The joint musical forces of KES and KEHS under Peter Bridle assembled in Birmingham Town Hall for the Christmas Concert, 1992. The Joint Orchestra gave concerts in Lyon in 1993.

Members of the Joint Orchestra entertain in an inner-city school. Ruth Wilkinson plays the horn and Kevin Greenbank the trumpet.

A group of senior masters bid farewell to the Quiet Room, sacrificed to rebuilding plans in 1987. It was the preserve of the elderly and known as the Geriatric Ward.

GAMES AND SPORTS

An outside view of the new swimming pool, opened in 1988.

The KES swimming team, 1957/58. From left to right, back row; Loach, Armstrong, Ellison, Hambridge. Front row: Tagg, McCarty, Davies, Bagnall.

Above: diving from the high board in the first swimming pool, the OE War Memorial gift, opened in 1952. Below: two simultaneous dives in 1978/79.

Martin Stead talks to a group of junior boys in the new swimming pool.

Action in the fives courts some time before they were roofed to enable play to take place in all weathers.

Fencing, presided over by John Cotter, was enthusiastically pursued at KES. Karl Hames and David Brewer engage in a bout, though who is who cannot be ascertained.

The range of school sports increased in the post-war years. Badminton was helped by the construction of the Sports Hall in 1971.

Hockey was introduced as a school game under the aegis of Bill Buttle in the late 1960s. The picture shows a KES XI of unspecified date, probably in the 1970s.

A combined U15 and U16 XI in action against a team of Peruvian boys in 1980/81.

Athletics at Eastern Road, *c.* 1910. The old pavilion seen here was demolished in 1965.

KES athletics team, 1949.

This runner in a relay race (in 1981) is either a long way ahead of the others, or a long way behind!

Pole vaulting at Eastern Road, 1977/78. The identity of the vaulter is uncertain (*cf.* p. 35).

KES basketball team in the ESBBA U19 Final, 1984. From left to right, back row: Ben Everson, Chris Grimley, Richard Chrimes, Kevin Withers, Warren Cowell, Iain Crawford, Stuart Birch. Front row: Julian Bishop, Jon Crawford, Alain Wolfe (captain), Andrew Crossley, Julian Crawford, Nick Willetts.

Chris Grimley seen in action in 1984 in the ESBBA final against Eastfield School. The following year he became basketball player of the year for the State of California.

KES players in action in 2000 against Baverstock School. Shalin Punn is the player with the ball.

Richard Chrimes and Chris Grimley of England Junior Men's basketball team, 1983/84.

Peter Jackson, OE (left 1947) about to side-step an opponent. He played for Coventry, Warwickshire, England and the British Lions.

Ian Metcalfe, OE (left 1977), playing for the England RFSU U19 against Wales at Cardiff. He subsequently played for Cambridge, the Barbarians and was an England tourist.

KES *v.* RGS Worcester, 1978. KES players in the foreground are Chris Roberts and Nick Merriman.

A house match. Elliott Simmonds is passing the ball, Tim Mason refereeing.

The Shells tasting 'manly sports'.

There was no time for shin-rubbing in this house match between Jeune and Cary Gilson.

KES first XV, 1996/97.

Ossie Wheatley, OE (left 1953), who played for Cambridge, Warwickshire and Glamorgan (of which he was captain and president), and was later chairman of the Cricket Committee of the TCCB.

Alan Smith, OE (left 1955), played for Oxford (as captain), Warwickshire and England (1961-62). He was Secretary of Warwickshire CCC and Chief Executive of the TCCB.

Paul Inglis (109 not out) and Neil Martin (148 not out) put on 270 for the first wicket against the Gentlemen of Worcester in 1987.

In 1997 the captain of each team in the University match was an OE. Mark Wagh and Anurag Singh subsequently both played for Warwickshire.

Cricket can continue all through the year in the indoor nets in the Sports Hall.

David Banks advises a very young cricketer in the important matter of grip.

KES XI, 1916. From left to right, back row: Prosser, Horsby, Caldicott, Richards, White, Clayton. Middle row: Whitehouse, Haughton, Boyton, Benson, Borrow. Front row: Moore (scorer), Carr (umpire).

KES first XI in 1953, one of the school's best sides. From left to right, back row: Max Wilkins, Alan Smith, Eric Saxon, Peter Mercer, Gordon Campbell, Jeremy Mulford. Front row: John Wilkins, Ossie Wheatley, Derek Benson (captain), Bryan Homer, Peter Simpson.

KES U12 XI, 1984.

KES first XI squad, 1997. From left to right, back row: Martin Stead, D.S. Payne, T.D.S. Owen, W.R.N. Webb, B. Muralidhar, G.H.A. Bhadr, R. Bera, R.J. Newman, A.M.H. Natkiel. Front row: N.Y. Khan, J.J. Child, R.J. McGuire, A.J. Martin (captain), A.D. Treharne, J.S. Ross.

Bob Willis, former Warwickshire and England fast bowler and England captain, with a group of young KES enthusiasts, 1981.

COMBINED CADET FORCE, SCOUTS AND OUTDOOR ACTIVITIES

A race in the Cadet Corps gymkhana at Eastern Road, probably in 1937.

Members of the RN Section, Vyse Company and Connnolly Company at HMS *Dolphin*, Gosport, 1978. Masters on parade are Lt Benson, Wing Cdr Traynor, Sub Lt Everest and Lt Stead, plus CPO Higgins and an unidentified RN lieutenant from *Dolphin*.

Above, Sub Lt Benett and the RN Section in the late 1940s; below, Lt Benson and the RN Section in the 1970s.

A group from the RN Section of the CCF visits HMS *Dolphin* in 1985. From left to right, back row: J. Duffy, N. Raj, K. Cunnane, R. Dudley, M. Hills, Lt Stead. Front row; C. Beighton, M. Potter, C. Counsell, J. Bishop.

The CCF band leads a march past KEHS, an attention not always appreciated when teaching was taking place on a Friday afternoon.

The Army Section parade on a sunny afternoon in 1981.

Dressing by the right outside the school chapel one Friday afternoon in 1983.

Standing easy in 1989.

Eagle Patrol, Park Vale Troop, near Betws-y-Coed, 1956. From left to right: Norman Henton, Mike Tracey, John Roberts, Tony Jackson and Roger Smith.

Scouts camping on Arran, 1959. Above, from left to right: Burgess, Hill, Bailey, Carmel and Gooch. Below, John Kent inspects unidentified junior boys.

Removes Field Week in Snowdonia in the 1980s.

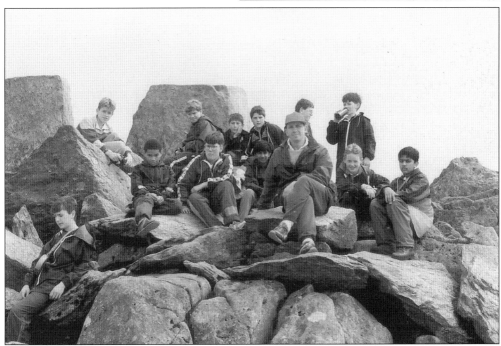

Removes Field Week. Ben Dunnett (later to be school captain) appears between the rocks. Foreground, in the cap, is Neil Gutteridge.

Owen Thomas absorbing the beauties of nature during Removes Field Week at Aberglaslyn, Snowdonia.

Canoeing during the Removes Expedition Week at Plas y Brenin, Snowdonia, 1993. On the extreme right is James Birch.

Rock climbers during Removes
Expeditions Week. On the right is
Dominic Cauldwell.

Rock climbing at a rather less relaxed
moment. The climber is Alex Brooke.

A KES party on a snow-walking jaunt in the Pyrenees, 1999. From left to right: Tristan Cox, Gregory Cooper, David Guest and the instructor, Pierre.

KES trekkers somewhere in the Alps on the Mont Blanc expedition in 1994. Leading the file is Nick Pilsbury.

Members of the KES expedition to Borneo in 2000 taking the air outside their long-house. From left to right: Ben Drew, Jamie Frew, Matt Carroll, Alex Lee, and Matt Clarke, with Tariq Arafa behind.

SOME MASTERS

H.W. ('George' or 'Buggy') Ballance (1924-1963), Head of Biology.

Harold Mayor (1952-1976), Head of Physics and Science Supremo (1952-1975), and Second Master (1970-1976).

Bernard Guy (1939-1979 except for war service, 1940-1946), Head of Chemistry (1946-1979), Science Supremo (1976-1979). Mr Guy was master in charge of cricket for two decades, and the finest batsman in Midlands club cricket.

George Andronov (1975-),
Head of Physics (1975-1997),
Science Supremo (1979-1997)
and Deputy Chief Master
(1997-).

David Rigby (1968-),
Head of Biology
(1977-) and
Science Supremo
(1997-).

The Common Room 1983.

The Common Room 1995.

The Prefects, 2002.

SECOND MASTERS

Rawdon Levett (1890-1902).

A.S. Langley (1934-1943),
Acting Headmaster (1941-1943).

E.V. Smith (1945-1970).

Harold Mayor (1970-1976).

John Hodges (1976-1981).

Roger Skinner (1981-1988), the last Second Master.

David Buttress (1988-1997), the first Deputy Chief Master.

George Andronov (1997-).

SOME OLD EDWARDIANS

J.R. Vane (left 1944), knight, Nobel
Prize Winner and Director of Group
Research and Development at the
Wellcome Research Laboratories.

Two controversial OEs. Left, J. Enoch Powell (left 1930), Professor of Greek, MP and Minister of Health; below, Ken Tynan (left 1945), *enfant terrible* at Oxford, brilliant dramatic critic, literary adviser to the National Theatre, and a powerful influence in the English theatre in the 1950s, '60s and '70s.

David Munrow (left 1960), an extraordinary musician and dynamic pioneer in the performance and dissemination of mediaeval and early Renaissance music. He was also a broadcaster and musicologist.

David Winkley (left 1960), knight, educationist, primary school headmaster, Fellow of Nuffield College, Oxford, founder and director of the National Primary Centre, and author.

Jonathan Coe (left 1980), novelist.

The Common Room, 2002.